Columbus
Indiana

A Look
At
Architecture

D1283971

Columbus Indiana

A Look At Architecture

Columbus
Indiana

A Look
At
Architecture

Copyright 1974, 1980
Columbus Area Chamber of Commerce, Inc.
All rights reserved
Published by Visitors Center, Columbus, Indiana

Arch.
NA
755
.C6?
C6Y
1980

The story of architecture in Columbus began generations ago when the foundation for a quality community, including buildings, was laid by farsighted city leaders in the mid-nineteenth century.

One building stands out—the Bartholomew County Courthouse, which dominates the city square. It has served the community well for 100 years with only minor alterations. In many ways it sets the pattern for architecture in Columbus—solid masonry, handsome and graceful. It is in daily use by residents of the county.

Another venerable building, the City Hall, has served continuously as the seat of city government since 1895. Still sturdy, its Victorian character intact, City Hall is being studied for renovation. Several other older buildings have been renovated in the downtown area.

In 1964 downtown merchants cooperated in storefront repainting and new signage for a "model block" between Fifth and Sixth Streets on Washington Street. This program was designed by Alexander Girard, an architect noted for his outstanding use of color. Since then many downtown area owners have followed the master plan to rejuvenate the typical Midwestern nineteenth century buildings.

Modern architecture began in Columbus with the First Christian Church, designed by Eliel Saarinen and dedicated in 1942. One of the earliest modern churches built in the United States, its simplicity and boldness have strongly influenced contemporary American church architecture. However, it was the need for new schools to accommodate population and industrial growth in the decade following World War II that provided the sustained thrust for the architectural program in Columbus. Only one new school had been constructed since 1929 for a population that had nearly doubled.

Cummins Engine Company, Inc., offered a unique proposal to the School Board Cummins Engine Foundation would pay architectural fees for new schools, with the stipulation that distinguished national architects be selected as the designers. Criteria indicated the School Board would have independent control of the project, design and budget, including selection of the architect from a list of at least six proposed by a panel of leading architects.*

The School Board accepted the program, and eleven schools have been constructed under this program, which later was to include other public buildings. A number of other buildings have been designed by noted architects without benefit of the Foundation plan, with building funds provided through contributions by congregations, bond issues, corporations, private funds, business and industry.

A redevelopment program for downtown Columbus, partially federally funded, provided a renewal for ten square blocks near the courthouse, with a two-block shopping and civic complex.

Columbus architecture has been the subject of feature articles in national and international publications, and each year thousands of people visit the city to view the buildings. In 1970, Columbus received the "Total Design" award from the National Society of Interior Design for exemplifying "environmental rebirth."

This guide book is printed by the Visitors Center, a division of the Columbus Area Chamber of Commerce, to enable visitors to learn more about Columbus buildings and the architects represented. Further information may be obtained from the Visitors Center. Trained volunteers serve as guides, and a guided tour by minibus is available. Reservations may be made at the Visitors Center, 506 Fifth Street, Columbus, Indiana 47201, telephone: 812-372-1954.

*Criteria more fully explained in Appendix, Page 107.

Chronological Listing

Alphabetical
Listing

Alphabetical
Listing

Columbus
Indiana

A Look
At
Architecture

1860

Bartholomew County Historical Museum
524 Third Street

Renovated in 1972

The Bartholomew County Historical Museum is located in the former home of three prominent early Columbus families.

The home was built by William McEwen, local businessman and banker. It was sold in 1870 to David Samuels and in 1889 to James Marr, a farmer, who with his family moved into the city. Upon his death in 1916, the house was divided into apartments and was allowed to deteriorate until purchased in 1969 by the Bartholomew County Historical Society for its headquarters and museum.

Restoration and renovation have returned the building to its prosperous appearance at the turn of the century, with the parlor decorated in Victorian period furniture. Other rooms display museum articles. There also is a historical reference room. A meeting room on the second floor is used for classes in the home arts, meetings and related activities.

1864

Visitors Center
Fifth and Franklin Streets

James Perkinson, Columbus
Renovated in 1973 by
Bruce Adams, New Haven, Connecticut

Increasing numbers of visitors attracted to the city's "showcase of modern architecture" determined the need for an information center, which is located in the former John Vawter Storey home, built in the period 1862-64. The historic house was purchased by the Cleo Rogers Memorial Library with funds made available by the Irwin-Sweeney-Miller Foundation in 1971. Mrs. J. Irwin Miller directed the renovation of the Storey house, completed in May, 1973.

The exterior of the Storey home has been restored with an addition on the back; the interior has been rebuilt to serve the needs of a visitors center and includes a display area upstairs.

In late 1974, the first branch outside Indianapolis of the Indianapolis Museum of Art was installed in the second story, with exhibits from its collection. "The Second Storey" is operated by volunteers from the Columbus Associates of the Indianapolis Museum of Art.

Occasionally, exhibits from memorabilia and archives of the architectural program in the city are presented.

The Visitors Center, a division of the Columbus Area Chamber of Commerce, operates a gift shop staffed by volunteers. Trained volunteers also provide guided tours.

1871

Senior Center
148 Lindsey Street

Renovated in 1976 by
James K. Paris, Columbus, Indiana

In 1975, when Community Development funds became available to Columbus, a series of public hearings was held, and a center for senior citizens was given top priority. The historic Power House on the banks of the White River was chosen as the site.

Now, after extensive repairs and renovation outside and inside, pinochle games, square dancing and Kitchen Band rehearsals have replaced the water pumps and dynamos that generated electric power for the city.

The Senior Center still has the 17-inch brick walls and stone foundation of two-foot thick slab put in during the 1901 renovation. Arches are the building's outstanding architectural feature, and two smaller arches, cut into existing interior walls, create a functional flow between rooms.

In the renovation an elevator was installed, and there are ramps instead of steps where feasible. A modern kitchen overlooks the falls in the river below.

In use every day and many evenings by the city's older citizens, the building also is used for varied community events.

1874

Bartholomew County Courthouse
Third and Washington Streets

Isaac Hodgson, Indianapolis, Indiana

Today the Courthouse stands much the same as it was at its completion in 1874. In 1928, 1953 and 1969, the building underwent interior renovation and repair.

Floors are marble and terrazzo; interior trim is wood, plaster and cast iron. Much of the original decor has been preserved, including fireplaces and a spiral staircase, although an elevator has been installed for convenience.

The building originally was roofed in slate, but was re-covered with copper in 1953, the first exterior change since 1874. The delicate, lightweight alloy grillwork on the three towers, to replace the original iron grillwork, was added in 1971, a gift of the late Miss Elsie Irwin Sweeney.

The building is said to have been the first fireproof building in Indiana. The architect, Isaac Hodgson, an Irish-born resident of Indianapolis, was one of nine charter members of the Indiana Chapter of the American Institute of Architects. He designed a number of courthouses and institutions throughout Indiana.

The renovation and repair of 1969 were under the direction of the county commissioners.

1895

City Hall
Fifth and Franklin Streets

Charles F. Sparrell, Columbus

Since 1895 this brick and limestone building has served the city of Columbus in a wide variety of ways: city government offices, police station, basketball court, ballroom, banquet hall, courtroom, market place and exhibit hall.

It is noteworthy that in the last decade of the nineteenth century there was extensive building in Columbus, an earlier "golden age" of architecture. The buildings have a sturdy Victorian character. A recent architectural survey of the City Hall, which is being considered for renovation, reads:

"Generally, all interior walls and floor systems are wood frame, still in reasonably good condition. The roof is entirely supported by large timber trusses, bearing on the exterior masonry walls. The stone foundation and brick masonry exterior walls show no indication of settlement or deterioration."

1942

First Christian Church
531 Fifth Street

Eliel Saarinen, Bloomfield Hills, Michigan

First Christian Church of Columbus was organized in 1855, and a brick Gothic building on Lafayette Street was built in 1878 during the pastorate of Reverend Z. T. Sweeney. In 1937, two members of the congregation, W. G. Irwin and his sister, Linnie I. Sweeney, the wife of Reverend Sweeney, presented the land where the First Christian Church now is located as a site for a new church.

Eliel Saarinen, chosen as the architect for the new church, suggested breaking away from traditional Gothic and Georgian styles. He wrote, "The last drop of expressiveness has been squeezed out of these once so expressive styles."

The First Christian Church, completed in 1942, was the first contemporary building in Columbus and one of the first contemporary churches in the United States. The geometric design is one of direct simplicity. The materials, exterior and interior, are mostly buff brick and limestone.

Above the main entrance a large stone cross accents the limestone facade of the massive rectangular building which is the sanctuary. Immediately to the west stands the 166-foot-high bell tower.

Inside the sanctuary, the counterpart of the outside cross highlights the south wall of the chancel. Beneath the cross there is a wall of wood accented with masses of growing ivy; a double gateway opens to reveal the baptistry pool.

On the east side of the chancel is the Aeolian-Skinner organ console with its 4,595 pipes concealed behind the wooden screen above it. In the center of the elevated chancel area stands the communion table. This sanctuary is 144 feet in length with a wide center aisle; the flat roof is 45 feet above.

Under the supervision of Mr. Saarinen, Charles Eames, then a young man, designed the furniture.

In the main building is a small chapel furnished in chestnut wood, and on the lower level are an auditorium, kitchen area and lounge. Between this larger building and a three-story classroom building on the west edge of the church complex, which covers a full city block, there is a two-story "bridge" supported on huge columns which form a lower level arcade with grassy terraces on either side. A pool which once reflected the tower has since been filled in.

Although the church is the oldest Columbus building of contemporary design, the simplicity and the dignity of its architecture make the First Christian Church one of the most admired buildings in the city.

1954

Irwin Union Bank & Trust Company
500 Washington Street

Eero Saarinen, Bloomfield Hills, Michigan

In designing the Irwin Union Bank, Eero Saarinen began with two major considerations: 1) to provide an efficiently functional structure for present-day banking, which would have dignity and yet reflect the friendly atmosphere of an old-fashioned country store, and 2) to maintain a compatible relationship of the new building to its 1910-era neighboring buildings.

The solution was found in a low, glass-walled structure in the middle of a tree-filled square. The trees were conceived as part of the architecture.

Common materials—brick, glass, and concrete—were used to maintain the spirit of modern, friendly banking. Limited use of interior partitions creates a large open room. The wide expanse of flat roof on the one-story building is interrupted by a series of shallow domes which house the interior lights. The bank tellers are not cloistered behind "cages," and there is easy access to other banking departments with several areas for comfortable, informal seating.

The concept of a landscaped park surrounding the bank was designed to integrate the bank with various types of neighboring buildings. The landscape architect, Dan Kiley of Charlotte, Vermont, selected littleleaf linden trees as a basis for that environment, adding euonymus as ground cover accented with seasonal plantings of spring bulbs, begonias and chrysanthemums.

1973

Irwin Union Bank & Trust Company Addition
Fifth and Jackson Streets

Kevin Roche John Dinkeloo
& Associates, Hamden, Connecticut

In 1973 a three-story adjacent building
to the north of the original bank was designed by Kevin Roche and John Dinkeloo.
Mr. Roche was Eero Saarinen's assistant
in the design of the original structure.

The most striking innovation of the new
addition is "striped" glass. It is a laminate
of two layers of glass, one sprayed in
stripes with a reflecting substance similar
to that used to back mirrors. This tech-
nique reduces the amount of heat absorbed
from the sun in the glass corridor which
runs the full block length from Washington
to Jackson Streets and rises the full
height of the addition.

This corridor is designed as a garden
arcade and contains copper-lined redwood
tubs containing ficus trees and seasonal
plantings such as mums and poinsettias.
Scattered benches add to the
garden setting.

1958

Irwin Union Bank & Trust Company
Hope Branch
East Side of Town Square, Hope, Indiana
Harry Weese, Chicago, Illinois

The rust-red brick branch bank building at
Hope was designed to fit a village square environment and features a glass clerestory, over
which "floats" the roof of pyramidal wooden
domes.

1961

Eastbrook Plaza Branch
25th Street and National Road
Harry Weese, Chicago, Illinois

The gray-glazed brick Eastbrook Plaza branch
bank building features four towers which combine
drive-up teller windows and heating and air-
conditioning units. Bordering on Hawcreek, the
building blends with two nearby bridges; a
small dam creates a reflecting pool.

1966

Taylorsville Branch, Taylorsville, Indiana
Fisher and Spillman Architects, Inc., Dallas, Texas

The branch bank at Taylorsville, eight miles
north of Columbus, is of rust-colored Louisiana
sandstone brick and glass and has been designed to harmonize with existing buildings of the
community and surrounding farm buildings,
which can be seen in the distance. The hip-type
roof is of copper with a large skylight.
The landscaping was planned by Dan Kiley of
Charlotte, Vermont.

1970

Columbus Center Branch
National Road
Donald G. Wood, Principal Architect
Taylor & Wood Architects
Columbus, Indiana

The low-profiled, beige brick Columbus Center
branch is accented by wide overhanging fascia
which wraps continuously around the entire
building. The off-white roof and the wide overhang
create a light, floating effect which accents the
clean, contemporary design. The interior complements the bank's subtle coloring with beige
carpeting and brown quarry tile flooring.

1974

State and Mapleton Streets Branch
Paul Kennon, Principal Architect
Caudill Rowlett Scott
Houston, Texas

The new State Street branch bank constructed in
1974 is a two-story masonry building with a
lobby glassed in on three sides. Four drive-up
teller windows are topped with plastic
bubbles above steel lattice work. The grounds
feature a tree-lined parking area and a landscaped mini-park.

1957

Lillian C. Schmitt Elementary School
1057 Twenty-Seventh Street

Harry Weese, Chicago, Illinois

Lillian C. Schmitt Elementary School,
including a kindergarten and twelve
classrooms, is a natural blend of brick,
glass and wood. The school, named
in honor of Miss Lillian Schmitt (1891-
1959), an elementary teacher in local
schools for 43 years, was the first in a
series of new schools named in honor of
local educators, and the first building
in the Cummins Engine Foundation architectural program.

Each room has a peaked roofline, making
an interesting zigzag exterior silhouette,
with ten classrooms opening directly onto
planned playground areas. In the middle
of the building a hexagonal multipurpose
room with a high ceiling can be enlarged
by opening folding doors into the main
corridor or into the cafeteria.

1958

Lincoln Center
2501 Twenty-Fifth Street

Harry Weese, Chicago, Illinois

This privately-endowed ice skating rink and recreational center is a gift to the Columbus community from the Hamilton Foundation as a memorial to B. F. Hamilton, founder of Cosco, Inc. The Foundation contributed this type of center because the community lacked recreational facilities for winter months.

Harry Weese was selected as architect because of his imagination and his philosophy of creating architectural beauty while fulfilling needs at the same time. He describes Lincoln Center: "The design is a kind of Black Forest stage setting for exhilarating evenings under the stars. But the daytime must also be considered — hence, the permanent natural materials, the opaqueness and the symmetry: all conspiring toward a civic, if informal, character."

The chalet-type building is of rough-hewn granite and glass with an interior-beamed, triple peaked roof. A circular granite fireplace, highlighting the spacious interior, is surrounded by wooden benches, an inviting sight to chilled skaters. The floor material is skate-resistant.

Because of an increased community interest in ice skating and the need to extend the skating season, the community decided to enclose the outdoor rink in 1975. Koster and Associates of Cleveland, Ohio, designed the new building as an extension of the existing center.

Now regulation hockey rink size, with an adjacent practice rink, the arena is available for off-season functions such as wedding receptions, business meetings, banquets, and auctions.

Lincoln Center and skating rink, with the nearby lighted tennis courts, baseball diamonds, handball courts, playgrounds and multi-purpose recreation area of Lincoln Park, are maintained by the Columbus Parks and Recreation Department and its board.

1959

Bartholomew County Home For The Aged
2525 Illinois Street

Harry Weese, Chicago, Illinois

This one-story building is a county-owned, state-licensed housing facility.
The east wing, housing the women in private rooms, and the similar west wing, housing the men, are connected by a comfortable lounge and dining area, with the kitchen and the manager's apartment behind the lounge.

The concrete block building with wood accents was financed by a county-wide bond issue. Landscaping was contributed by the Hamilton Foundation.

1960

Mabel McDowell Elementary School
2700 McKinley Avenue

John Carl Warnecke, San Francisco,
California

Mabel McDowell Elementary School
clusters four pagoda-type classroom
buildings around an inner grouping
of buildings, with a landscaped courtyard
in the center.

The center buildings contain a multipurpose room, offices, kindergarten and
cafeteria. The four corner buildings, each
containing three classrooms, are connected to the nucleus buildings by trellis-
covered walkways, with landscaped
patios between.

The steel-frame, brick buildings are
covered with shingled roofs, which create
deep eaves to shade the large expanses
of windows. Each of the classroom units
has a storage area and rest rooms.

Architect John Carl Warnecke said of the
area and school, "A dominant charac-
teristic of Southern Indiana is the flat ter-
rain, a horizontal theme accentuated by
tall Victorian houses, barns and silos, with
picturesque groves of trees. The school
design is based on the creation of a similar grouping of masses and spaces into
a scheme which focuses the school group
into its own controlled environment, yet
extends it outward into the community."

This school is named in honor of Miss
Mabel McDowell (1880-1961), elementary
school teacher in Columbus for 25 years.

1961

Northside Junior High School
2700 Maple Street

Harry Weese, Chicago, Illinois

Distinguishing feature of this massive building is its repetitive use of brick arches, most of them inset with windows.

A landscaped interior courtyard has been offset from the center of the building. The gymnasium multipurpose room, often used for community events, and the regulation-size swimming pool are placed side by side, with entry from either the courtyard corridor or street side entrances.

The hallways are lined with lockers, with glass-inset arches above allowing natural light to filter into the halls from the classrooms. The building houses 28 regular classrooms and 17 special use rooms.

Administrative offices are located just inside the main entrance, with the library located on the top floor overlooking the courtyard; the cafeteria is on the lower floor.

Architect Harry Weese has described this building as "a firm statement of the dignity and prominence in the community that a school should possess."

1962

Cosco, Inc. Office Building
2525 State Street

Harry Weese, Chicago, Illinois

With the growth of Cosco, Inc., came a
need for more office and research space.
In 1962, Harry Weese, who designed
the Lincoln Center facility for the Hamilton
Foundation, was asked to redesign the
industrial company facilities as well as
to add a new research facility. The brick
and glass additions are functional and
pleasant.

The landscape architect, Dan Kiley of
Charlotte, Vermont, selected a variety of
trees, including ginkgo, river birch, horn-
beam and oak, as well as yews and a
groundcover of euonymus.

1962

Parkside Elementary School
1400 Parkside Drive

The Architects Collaborative, Inc.,
Boston, Massachusetts
Norman Fletcher, Principal Architect

Identifying feature of Parkside Elementary School is the series of barrel-vaults, presenting an umbrella effect, first seen in the school bus loading shelter in front of the school. The same architectural device is repeated in the central multi-purpose section used as cafeteria, gymnasium and meeting room.

The school is on a two-foot podium of earth, with recessed court and play areas, to provide a change of experience from the otherwise flat landscape.

The design of this school utilizes an educational approach emphasizing the individual within his or her own age group. The lower and upper grades are housed in separate wings, each with an outdoor courtyard. In the upper grades' wing there is also a "students' forum," adaptable for audio-visual aids, several classes meeting together or dramatizations. It is encircled with graduated steps utilized for seating.

In the courtyard in front of the central section stands "The Family" sculpture, a gift to the community schools by Mrs. J. Irwin Miller through the Columbus School Foundation. Three angular figures represent a father, mother and child. Its creator is Harris Barron of Brookline Village, Massachusetts; the sculpture is carved from Chelmsford granite.

1963

Bartholomew Consolidated School
Corporation
Administration Building
2650 Home Avenue

The Architects Collaborative, Inc.,
Boston, Massachusetts
Norman Fletcher, Principal Architect

This octagonal brick building, in the
midst of the city's major school complex,
serves as headquarters for the administration of the Bartholomew Consolidated
School Corporation.

Windows, separated by brick pediments,
extend the full height of the two-story
building. The lobby features a curved staircase set against a curved brick wall
rising in the center of the building. Administrative offices fan out and surround
this center.

The roof peaks above the stairwell. The
eight-paneled glass dome allows natural
light to highlight the interior.

The Board of Trustees of the Bartholomew
Consolidated School Corporation was
recognized by the Indiana Arts Commission in 1973 for accepting the challenge
of the community to build better schools.

1964

North Christian Church
850 Tipton Lane

Eero Saarinen, Bloomfield Hills, Michigan

Eero Saarinen, the son of architect Eliel Saarinen, chosen as the architect for this church, worked closely with members of the congregation to understand the church's theology, traditions and expectations as well as its leadership in the growing concept of an ecumenical faith.

This is the last building designed by Eero Saarinen before his untimely death. While planning the building, he wrote to the congregation: "We have finally to solve this church so that it can become a great building. I feel I have this obligation to the congregation, and as an architect I have that obligation to my profession and my ideals. I want to solve it so that as an architect when I face St. Peter I am able to say that out of the buildings I did during my lifetime, one of the best was this little church, because it has in it a real spirit that speaks forth to all Christians as a witness to their faith."

The sloping roof of this hexagonal building blends with the landscaped earth mound which surrounds it. This low line accentuates the slender 192-foot spire, topped with a gold leaf cross, which gives North Christian Church its distinctive design.

The church interior is designed to make the sanctuary the center of the church and the communion table the center of the sanctuary, as it is the focal point of the worship service. On a tiered platform, the communion table is comprised of twelve pedestal tables symbolic of the twelve disciples. At one end is a higher pedestal — the Christ table, which holds a silver chalice and a loaf of bread, the communion elements, for services.

Opposite the main entrance are the pulpit, choir loft and a Holtkamp organ, the last organ designed by Walter Holtkamp, Sr. The installation was worked out in close cooperation with the architect.

Direct natural light enters the sanctuary through an oculus high in the ceiling at the base of the spire, and other natural lighting is diffused from under the edge of the roof line.

There is a chapel to the west of the sanctuary with emphasis on the baptismal pool. Classrooms and offices encircle the sanctuary.

On the lower level there are an auditorium, lounge, youth activities area, music area kitchen and classrooms.

1964

Otter Creek Clubhouse and Golf Course
County Road 50 North

Harry Weese, Chicago, Illinois (Clubhouse)
Robert Trent Jones, Montclair, N. J.
(Golf Course)
Dan Kiley, Charlotte, Vermont
(Landscaping)

As one approaches Otter Creek Clubhouse
and Golf Course, located five miles east
of Columbus, the first impression is of the
compatibility of the building and its setting. The modern-rural feeling of the building is achieved in the extensive use of
wood, and the precision of its geometric
patterns complements the orderliness
of the 18-hole golf course.

The glass-walled clubhouse was designed
by Harry Weese. It includes spacious
lounge and dining areas; porches over-
look the golf course.

World-famous Robert Trent Jones has
called this golf course one of his best. The
7,094 yard championship course has
72 bunkers and seven water hazards.
The course has been designed to test
the ability of the expert and yet remains
within the capability of the average golfer.
Double rows of littleleaf linden trees line
the driveway leading to a circular pool and
fountain before the main entrance. Dan
Kiley of Charlotte, Vermont, was the
landscape architect.

Otter Creek Clubhouse and Golf Course
were given to the city of Columbus by
Cummins Engine Company, Inc., on June
21, 1964.*

*See Appendix Page 108 for the dedication remarks of
 J. Irwin Miller.

1965

First Baptist Church
3300 Fairlawn Drive

Harry Weese, Chicago, Illinois

The First Baptist Church is built on the brow of a gently sloping knoll. This elevation, combined with its peaked nondimensional bell tower, inspires a liturgical impression. The steep roof, which is twice as high as the supporting pink brick walls, is covered with hand-laid slate.

The sanctuary has a high A-frame interior. Highlight of the interior design is a wall of pierced brick at the front of the church. This wall partially screens the choir, organ and baptistry from the congregation. The off-center aisle leads to the communion table. All elements in the design are off-center except the sanctuary cross, which appears to float in mid-air. A vertical row of glass panels, piercing the steeply sloping roof above the chancel, gives natural lighting to the cross.

The chapel is in a smaller, separate, but similar building to one side of the sanctuary.

The main brick building is built on two levels, taking advantage of a natural grade, around a landscaped open courtyard. Classrooms are on the first floor, with the sanctuary, chapel and fellowship room on the second.

1965

W. D. Richards Elementary School
3311 Fairlawn Drive

Edward Larrabee Barnes, New York,
New York

W. D. Richards Elementary School features bold sloping roofs forming serrated silhouettes. The distinctive high spine of this school building is created by the set of four 28-foot high clerestories above the multipurpose gymnasium/cafeteria in the center of the school. There are parallel corridors on each side of the center room and smaller clerestories serve classrooms.

The purpose of these roof-jutting, skylight arrangements is to provide maximum natural studio-type lighting and additional wall space in the classrooms. Each of six grades is housed in a three-room cluster. Each room has its own outside exit opening onto small plaza areas. Porthole windows in the classroom doors and other appointments are at child height. Wings forming the entry terrace accommodate the kindergarten area on one side, offices and library on the other.

The front entrance of the school, facing west, opens onto a recessed terrace planted with eight magnolia trees. Dan Kiley of Charlotte, Vermont, was the landscape architect.

The elementary school is named for William Dalbert Richards (1884-1957), native of Bartholomew County, who served as teacher and principal in Columbus elementary schools for 45 years.

The main playground is located behind the school. Twelve sculptured miniature horses, a gift of Mrs. J. Irwin Miller and created by Costantino Nivola, a Sicilian artist working in New York City, invitingly encircle a huge ash tree.

1966

Foundation For Youth
400 North Cherry Street

Fisher and Spillman Architects, Inc.,
Dallas, Texas

Columbus Foundation for Youth organization includes the Boys Club and Girls
Club, also the rustic Youth Camp in the hill
country west of Columbus, a 115-acre
gift of Mr. and Mrs. Q. G. Noblitt.

The first part of the three-building group
on North Cherry Street was used by both
the Boys Club and Girls Club and was
designed by Harry Weese in 1954. When
major remodeling was undertaken, this
earlier building became the Girls Club, and
it was redesigned to conform with the
new buildings, including the addition of a
multi-peaked roofline.

This building is connected by a covered
walkway to the taller center building,
large enough to accommodate two gymnasium areas and a regulation-size
swimming pool. On the other side, also
connected by a covered walk, is the
multi-peaked Boys Club.

1967

Four Seasons Retirement Center
1901 Taylor Road

The Architects Collaborative, Inc.,
Boston, Massachusetts
Norman Fletcher, Principal Architect

There are 114 apartments in this senior citizen complex built on one level, with each having a private patio and a small garden area. They also open onto common corridors which interconnect all of the center's wings. It is managed by Baptist Homes & Hospitals, Inc., with a staff of 95, including two full-time activities directors.

Located within the complex are a beauty shop, barber shop, snack bar and gift shop, library, dining area, lounges and a health center.

The spacious central dining and lounge area has a sunken courtyard planted with living trees and plants under skylights. Besides the lobby and center core lounge, there are smaller lounge areas where corridors join.

In a separate but connected building, there is a wood and brick A-frame chapel with skylights at the high peak of the roof, which rises high above the other buildings in the complex.

1967

Fire Station No. 4
State Road 46, East

Venturi & Rauch, Philadelphia,
Pennsylvania

The No. 4 Fire Station of Columbus Fire
Department is built in a trapezoidal shape
of cinderblock, white glazed and red
unglazed brick and glass. The building is
divided into five basic areas—garage,
kitchen, lounge, sleeping area and the
unique hose-drying tower.

The hose-drying tower provides a focal
point against an otherwise low, utilitarian
building.

1967

Lincoln Elementary School
750 Fifth Street

Gunnar Birkerts, Birmingham, Michigan

In discussing the philosophy of his Lincoln School design, Gunnar Birkerts states, "School is not a building . . . it is an activity . . . it begins at the sidewalk . . . it is an educational area . . . designed to stimulate, challenge or arouse curiosity."

A "bird's eye" view of Lincoln School would be a square within a circle within a square. The square two-story brick building is encircled with a low retaining wall and a ring of littleleaf linden trees. Play area of the younger children is within this circle, close to the school. The main playground, for the older children, is outside the circle and to the north end of the block, which is bordered with grassy earthworks on four sides, serving as bunkers between the school and streets.

The school is actually a building within a building. In the center the independent multipurpose room is constructed of tongue-and-groove birch walls with laminated wood beams and columns. The "outer-building" is constructed of brick and concrete.

Corridors surround the multipurpose room on both levels with doorways leading into classrooms, which are carpeted, and into special purpose rooms. From the second floor corridor, students can look over a parapet topped with narrow, slanted glass windows into the central core room below. Two roof systems are joined by a three-foot wide clerestory, or skylight, on all sides of the building, infusing natural light into the core room and the corridors.

In September 1967, Mrs. Lyndon B. Johnson, wife of the President of the United States, on her "Crossroads U.S.A." tour commemorated her visit to Columbus by dedicating a plaque at the entrance to the school.

Lincoln School received an AIA Honor Award in 1968.

1968

Cummins Engine Company, Inc.,
Technical Center
1900 McKinley Avenue

Harry Weese, Chicago, Illinois

Cummins Engine Company Technical
Center, designed by Harry Weese, incorporates two connecting buildings, a
six-story, window-wall office section for
the professional engineering staff and
a two-story research and engine testing
facility.

Both buildings are constructed of steel,
glass and concrete. The research and
engine testing facility utilizes modular,
pre-cast concrete panels to create the
exterior curtain wall, a method used in
several other Cummins buildings constructed since 1957.

In contrast, the concrete of the six-story
office building was poured floor by floor.
Oblong pre-cast concrete sun shades
are attached outside the glass exterior.

A unique feature of the building is the
ceiling design of pre-cast concrete which
incorporates all electrical and mechanical systems, thus eliminating extensive wiring and heating duct installation.

The area around the Technical Center
has been landscaped with trees, grass,
pools and plantings, designed by Dan
Kiley of Charlotte, Vermont, including the
rows of London plane trees lining Hawcreek Boulevard and the planting around
the main plant and the medical center.

1969

Cleo Rogers Memorial Library
536 Fifth Street

I. M. Pei and Partners, New York,
New York

Cleo Rogers Memorial Library was designed by architect I. M. Pei, chosen for his total concept and concern for the proper location of the library—that it occupy a space which would be quiet yet dignified; that it be out of the flow of heavy traffic; that it be easily accessible to the great majority of people, both young and old; that its location create an area of urban space; that it take into consideration the future growth of the community and its character.

Mr. Pei recommended the closing of Lafayette Street between Fifth and Sixth Streets to create a viable public space, featuring in addition to the Library and "Large Arch," the First Christian Church and bell tower and the Irwin Home.

The library building is a brick pavilion with solid walls on the east and west. The main entrance vestibule is located off center at the west end of the front of the building on Fifth Street; long windows are deeply recessed. There are two enclosed walled terraces included in the plan. The Children's Library is on the lower level with its own entrance to the west.

The main reading room is at the west end of the building. The lofty coffered concrete ceiling also serves acoustical, lighting and heating purposes. The balcony mezzanine is used for displays and administrative offices.

The reference library, with carrels for individual study, is at the east end of the building, and service desks and card catalogues are between the two main departments on the main floor. Immediately to the right of the main entrance is a small gallery, used for local or special art displays.

On the east end of the lower level, there is a community use area with meeting rooms, kitchenette, restrooms, coat room area and lobby, with outside entrance.

A driveway curves in front of the library, and in the center circle stands "Large Arch," a major work of English sculptor Henry Moore.

Sidewalk art shows are presented each spring and fall, and there have been many outdoor concerts in the plaza area.

1969

L. Frances Smith Elementary School
4505 Waycross Drive

John M. Johansen, New Canaan,
Connecticut

Eye-catching exterior features of the
L. Frances Smith Elementary School are
the seven brightly painted steel ramps
or "tubes" connecting the multi-levels of
the reinforced concrete and Cor-ten
steel structure. Cor-ten has a high tin content and soon builds up a surface rust,
which becomes a permanent rich brown
color.

The building was planned for three educational complexes, each with space for
six classes of about 30 students each. On
the lowest level are the cafeteria, gymnasium, art and music rooms and kindergarten.

The tubes, or tunnels, slope gently upward
to the next level, the lower primary complex, then move onward and upward to the
upper primary and intermediate complex
levels. The top floor contains a learning resource center with library, audio-visual
materials, special study area and work-
rooms.

Ceilings, walls and floors of the tubes are
carpeted, creating excellent art display
areas as well as providing noise control.

This school was named in honor of Miss
L. Frances Smith (1901-1971), super-
visor of elementary education in Columbus
schools for 24 years, who had been a
teacher for ten years before she held
that position.

1969

Southside Junior High School
County Road 200 South,
off U.S. 31A

Eliot Noyes, New Canaan, Connecticut

Southside Junior High School has jutting
parapets and unusual window and door
treatment. The interior and exterior walls
of pre-cast concrete, reinforced concrete and concrete blocks have been allowed to remain in a natural state
without paint or other finishing materials.

The main entrance opens onto the "commons" in the center of the school under a
two-story skylight area.

To the left of the entrance is a 400-seat
auditorium which can be divided into
three areas by two sound-proof movable
partitions. The lower level has a gymnasium, swimming pool and industrial arts
classrooms.

Large abstract murals designed by Ivan
Chermayeff of New York City and commissioned by Mr. and Mrs. J. Irwin Miller,
add bright color to the stairwell walls.

1970

Columbus Post Office
450 Jackson Street

Kevin Roche John Dinkeloo & Associates,
Hamden, Connecticut

The Columbus Post Office is built of a
special salt-glazed tile, mirrored glass
and Cor-ten steel and is relatively
maintenance free. The salt-glazed tile,
commonly used in silos, was espe-
cially glazed reddish-brown to match the
color of the Cor-ten.

The decorative mirrored-glass walls and
doors on the front of the building provide
interesting reflections. From the inside
this special glass is transparent. Massive,
tile-covered, square pillars form an
arcade over the sidewalk on Jackson
Street. High ceilings lend an air of
spaciousness to the entire building.

It is one of two post offices in the nation to
include a congressional office, that of
Indiana Ninth District Congressman in the
House of Representatives, and it was the
first designed by privately-paid architects.

1971

Sculpture: Large Arch
Library Plaza

Sculptor: Henry Moore, Much Hadham, Hertfordshire, England

Henry Moore's sculpture, "Large Arch," which centers the Cleo Rogers Memorial Library plaza, was commissioned at the suggestion of I. M. Pei of New York City, architect for the library. He wanted Henry Moore, considered one of the greatest artists of the twentieth century, to create the plaza centerpiece. Mr. Moore, who was 77 years old when he did the "Large Arch," said, "As a young sculptor I saw Stonehenge and ever since I've wanted to do work that could be walked through and around."

The organic quality of the "Large Arch" is a direct contrast to the geometric shapes of the nearby buildings. It reflects primitive simplicity and the power evident in monolithic sculpture of the past. It is twenty feet tall, twelve feet wide and weighs five and a half tons.

It was designed in Mr. Moore's studio at his home in England and sandcast in bronze in fifty sections at the Herman Noack foundry in West Germany. The pieces, one-fourth to one-half inch thick, were welded with invisible seams. The green patina is a natural aged-look for bronze, if in a climate free of air impurities, and was created through a special process, directed personally by Mr. Moore at the foundry.

The sculpture, a gift from Mr. and Mrs. J. Irwin Miller, was dedicated with the library building, May 16, 1971.

1971

The Republic
333 Second Street

Skidmore, Owings & Merrill,
Chicago, Illinois
Myron Goldsmith, Design Partner

The plan of The Republic newspaper plant implements the flow of material for both the advertising and editorial content of the paper from the west end of the glass-walled building to the final product, a daily newspaper, with the printing press and distribution area on the east.

The interior is highly visible from the street, and a bright yellow offset press in a prominent location contributes a powerful modern sculpture.

Two long high-ceilinged areas on the south and north are joined by a center core of low-ceilinged offices and work areas. The editorial and circulation departments are on the south, the advertising and composing departments sharing the north with the pressroom. Administrative offices are located on the west end of the building.

All interior walls and partitions are white, several accented with contemporary art, and all floors are carpeted except in the pressroom, circulation and service areas.

The Republic building received an AIA Honor Award in 1975.

1972

Par 3 Golf Course Clubhouse
Fairlawn at Par 3 Drive

Bruce Adams, New Haven, Connecticut

During the summer of 1972 this clubhouse
was built of rough lumber. The challenge
was to be a good design neighbor to the
nearby First Baptist Church and Richards
School. The clubhouse includes a professional shop, lounge, rest rooms and
storage space.

Over 15,000 rounds of golf are played
annually on this eighteen hole, par 3 course.
Constructed in 1966, the 45-acre Par 3
Golf Course is landscaped with crabapple,
blue spruce, Scotch pine and pin oaks.

Par 3 is an excellent facility for young
golfers to learn the game; it is ideally
suited for leisure play and also for
senior citizens.

1972

Mt. Healthy Elementary School
State Road 58

Hardy Holzman Pfeiffer Associates,
New York, New York

This school is the first rural Bartholomew
County school built under the Cummins
Engine Foundation architectural program,
and the first under an open classroom
teaching plan.

A symbolic return to the one-room schoolhouse, this building celebrates the variety
inherent in open planning. There are few
complete enclosures or doors.

The school is built of several dissimilar
materials deliberately set in geometric
juxtapositions, and this construction
creates a wide range of teaching
environments.

Three multi-level clusters are used by the
primary, upper primary and intermediate
classes. There are no doorways except at
the passageways leading into the gymnasium and the music room.

A "spine" corridor connects all areas of
the building, and offset patterns of roof
and wall glazing assure that no two
clusters have the same enclosure.

1972

Quinco Consulting Center
2075 Lincoln Park Drive

James Stewart Polshek, New York,
New York

"Quinco" was the name chosen for this consulting center, the culmination of a six-year combined effort of five area counties to achieve an effective program for dealing with problems of mental health. Designed by James Stewart Polshek, the building's decisive design element is that it spans Hawcreek. On one bank is the Bartholomew County Hospital and on the other, a city park.

The two-story building plan is based on two offset rectangles, with the main lounge at the broad middle section and a balcony bridge on the second floor above it.

On the second floor, out-patient facilities with staff offices are on one side of the lounge bridge. On the other side is the 26-bed in-patient center with day room.

An outstanding feature of the center is the unusual angled glass panels which incorporate a skylight effect in the second-floor windows.

The center also is used for training and research and serves as a base of operations for outlying clinics in all five counties.

This facility and its services are largely the result of the efforts of Lowell Engelking, first president of the Bartholomew County Mental Health Association.

1972

Columbus East Senior High School
230 South Marr Road

Mitchell-Giurgola Associates,
Philadelphia, Pennsylvania

The architects were given the challenge by the school administration to prepare a high school building to fit a program which could house flexible modular scheduling and team teaching.

The heart of the building is the two-story gallery level which includes a "commons" and cafeteria, with a wall of glass opening onto a terrace. The main floor, which has a half wall above the commons area and lower level corridor, includes the offices, bookstore and five large group instruction rooms.

The second floor is totally academic, containing resource centers and laboratories. The open areas on the second floor enhance the concept that exposure to other subjects will generate wider interests.

The third floor of this building is a series of small discussion rooms for about fifteen students each. They are directly above the resource centers for the easy transportation of instructional material. The whole school program emphasizes individual study with faculty guidance.

There is a 900-seat auditorium at one end of the school and a 4,200-seat gymnasium at the other.

Special features incorporated by the architects include a swimming pool, a planetarium, a specially equipped industrial arts wing, a greenhouse and an animal room for the science classes.

East Senior High School received an AIA Honor Award in 1975.

1973

Columbus Occupational Health
Association
605 Cottage Avenue

Hardy Holzman Pfeiffer Associates,
New York, New York

This clinic is a new concept in industrial
medicine — serving employees of 109
companies in the community. Departing
from the traditional antiseptic role of a
clinic, this Occupational Health Center
has been designed with lots of glass
and few walls.

The exterior is sheathed in black glass
cut at a 45° angle by a mirrored glass
entryway and skylight.

Public circulation is based upon a split-
level scheme in which all medical functions
surround a large open waiting space. This
open volume is bisected by two gently
sloping ramps which connect the three
half-levels of the building and give access
to all medical functions, many of which
are open to public view. Corridor circulation between activities is left open, and
interspersed throughout are semicircular
seating pods. A second, more private,
vertical circulation system of staircases
is used primarily for patients and staff
during examination and treatment.

COHA received an AIA Honor Award
in 1976.

1973

Fodrea Community School
2775 Illinois Street

Caudill Rowlett Scott
Paul Kennon, Truitt Garrison, Principal
Architects, Houston, Texas

This "people-centered" school is one of
the first in the country to be designed as a
community center as well as a school.
It is the third Columbus school designed in
the open-classroom concept for team
teaching, with three "learning areas," two
kindergarten areas and several special
use areas. It offers elementary education,
adult education, children-adult recreation
and community-civic organization space.

The architects from the firm of Caudill
Rowlett and Scott, with Paul Kennon and
Truitt Garrison in charge, incorporated
suggestions made by the children who at-
tended the school and by members of the
community at a series of open meetings.

One feature of the school is a public con-
course leading to an open space in the
center of the school planted with grass and
trees. This area always will be accessible
to passersby or visitors.

This school was named for three sisters,
Miss Hazel Fodrea, Miss Bess Fodrea and
Mrs. Mabel Fodrea Jordan, who taught
a total of 84 years in community schools.

Fodrea was chosen as one of 32 schools
out of 350 entries to be shown in a filmstrip
of outstanding design in school architecture at the 1973 American Association
of School Administrators.

1973

Commons-Courthouse Center
Fourth and Washington Streets

Gruen Associates, Inc.,
Los Angeles, California
Cesar Pelli, Principal Architect

Due to the growth of Columbus and the deterioration of the downtown area, a basic urban renewal plan was begun with federal funds to clear and rebuild a 53-acre area, one fourth of the downtown area.

The city commissioned the architectural and engineering firm of Skidmore, Owings and Merrill to prepare a detailed, long-range development plan for downtown Columbus, including traffic and parking proposals and landscaping. The three major objectives were relocating major railroad tracks, construction of two one-way main arteries carrying through traffic around the downtown area and developing a major shopping complex downtown.

A two-block area bounded by Brown, Washington, Third and Fourth Streets was designated as a "super-block" for a shopping center. Jackson Street between Third and Fourth was closed for this project.

Irwin Management Company, Inc. purchased the super-block and surrounding parking area. Announcement of an enclosed shopping mall was made in March, 1972.

Mr. and Mrs. J. Irwin Miller and his sister, Mrs. Robert Tangeman, gave to the city a Civic Mall in the front part of the complex facing Washington Street, serving as a hinge between the new shopping facilities and the already existing shops. This mall (named The Commons) is a public space and includes an exhibit hall, stage, playground with built-in "play tank," two movie theaters, a restaurant, snack bar, several meeting rooms and a general information center.

The Commons also is headquarters for the Driftwood Valley Arts Council, which sponsors a variety of cultural activities for the community.

The entire complex, all under cover, is enclosed with brown glass with large expanses of clear glass on the Washington Street side. In addition to the Sears store (the project's major retail generator which opened in March of 1973), the shopping mall has space for fifteen to twenty shops. A mini-mall includes several small boutiques. A total of three square blocks of parking area serves the center.

1974

Sculpture: Chaos I
The Commons

Sculptor: Jean Tinguely,
Zurich, Switzerland

A highlight of The Commons is the "in motion" sculpture, "Chaos I," created by Jean Tinguely. In recommending a major work of art for The Commons, Cesar Pelli, architect, stated, "We would like a great magnet, a focal point such as the old town clock . . . a place for people to meet and greet one another."

"Chaos I," like much of Mr. Tinguely's work, is fabricated from scrap metal. Most of the materials for its construction were purchased locally, and the sculpture was fabricated with the aid of local craftsmen working under Mr. Tinguely's direction. "Chaos I" is approximately 30 feet high and weighs almost seven tons.

Jean Tinguely is well known for his motion sculpture. During his first American show at the Museum of Modern Art in 1960, one of the featured works was the now famous "Homage to New York." "Homage," which destroyed itself (with the aid of some willing New York firemen armed with axes), is a prime example of the great delight and humor Mr. Tinguely sees in his work.

The sculptor sees "Chaos I" as one of his best works. It represents one of Mr.Tinguely's most important ideas about art: "Life is movement. Everything transforms itself, everything modifies itself ceaselessly, and to try to stop it . . . seems to me a mockery of the intensity of life."

"Chaos I" was commissioned by Mrs. Robert Tangeman and Mr. and Mrs. J. Irwin Miller.

1973

Cummins Engine Company, Inc.,
Components Plant
Off Interstate 65—Walesboro Community

Kevin Roche John Dinkeloo and
Associates, Hamden, Connecticut

This building spreads out under thirteen
and one-half acres of roof with parking
thereon.

The main floor of the building is actually
two levels. The manufacturing floor is
three feet lower than the office areas which
surround three sides. The complex was
designed to increase productivity and flexibility of manufacturing. Cummins had
as one of its main goals the preservation
and enhancement of surroundings for
those employed in the facility.

As a result, special attention has been given
to creating an environmentally controlled
system which adds air, noise and water-
pollution control devices that surpass stand-
ards anticipated for the future. The layout
of the plant gives all of the over 2,000
employees a view of the outside.

In the middle of the manufacturing area is
a landscaped courtyard completely surrounded by glass. Cafeterias are located
in the southeast and northwest corners
of the building. Both have treated walls
and slanted glass roofs.

This Kevin Roche factory design has been
acclaimed as a prototype of future factory
buildings. A model was on exhibit at the
Museum of Modern Art in New York City in
1970 in a 3-man architectural display
entitled, "Work in Progress: Architecture
by Philip Johnson, Kevin Roche, Paul
Rudolph." The 25 exhibits were of buildings under construction at that time.

1978

Indiana Bell Telephone Company
Switching Center
Seventh and Franklin Streets

Caudill Rowlett Scott
Houston, Texas
Paul Kennon, Design Principal
Jay Bauer, Designer

The architect's challenge was to design an addition for an existing commercial building on a transitional site, joining the business district and one of the community's older, but viable residential areas.

The solution was to unify the existing building and the new addition by encasing both in a skin of reflecting glass. The result is a "non-building" which mirrors activities of the surrounding neighborhood.

The visual impact is softened by a two-story trellis wall of greenery — ivy, wisteria and climbing hydrangeas.

Giant yellow, red and blue "organ pipes" on the west side of the building provide a colorful accent. Functional as well as decorative, they house and camouflage the air conditioning and heating units.

Indiana Bell Telephone Switching Center received an AIA Honor Award in 1980.

Renovations

A growing awareness and appreciation of the community's quality architectural heritage are visible in the storefront improvements and creative renovations of both exterior and interior spaces in the downtown area. A major community goal, with continuing emphasis, is the preservation and revitalization of the historic center city, the governmental, financial and services "heart" of Columbus. The following buildings are representative.

1
Irwin Gardens
2
Irwin Management Company
3
Zaharako's Confectionery
4
Professional Offices
5
Downtown Storefront Improvements
6
Franklin Square Interiors
7
Franklin Square Offices
8
Law Offices
9
Irwin Block
10
St. Bartholomew Roman Catholic Church

1

2

3

4

5

8

6

9

7

10

Architectural
Awareness

Visitors to Columbus frequently ask, "Has the quality of major buildings had any impact on other construction in the community?" The answer is, "Yes," as evidenced by the large number of homes, churches and private businesses that have been professionally designed, landscaped and decorated. Among the creative talents residing and working in Columbus are a number of architects, landscape architects and interior designers.

These are illustrative of the growing community appreciation for the benefits of quality construction and works of art.

1
Bartholomew County Governmental Offices
2
Sandy Hook United Methodist Church
3
Sculpture: Skopos
4
Goodyear Service Center
5
Citizens Savings and Loan Association
6
Asbury United Methodist Church

1

2

3

4

5

6

Future

As this edition of "A Look At Architecture" was being readied for publication, several new buildings either were under construction or in the final stages of design. Construction of the new City Hall began in 1979, with completion scheduled for 1981. Groundbreaking for the new Clifty-Petersville Elementary School was planned for mid-1980. In support of the downtown Columbus revitalization program, Cummins Engine Company has announced plans for its world headquarters building in the central area. The building will occupy approximately three blocks and house 1,000 office and management personnel.

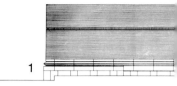
1

1
Columbus City Hall
Charles Bassett, Principal Architect,
Skidmore, Owings & Merrill
Chicago, Illinois

2
Cummins Engine Company, Inc.,
Headquarters
Kevin Roche John Dinkeloo and Associates
Hamden, Connecticut

3
Clifty-Petersville Elementary School
Richard Meier and Associates
New York, New York

2

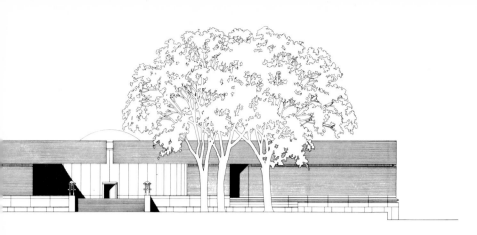

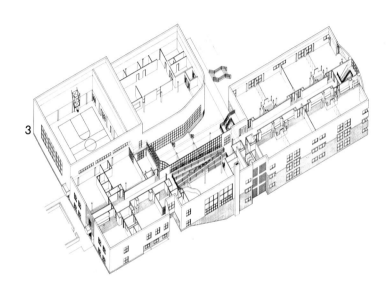

3

103

Cummins Engine Foundation Architectural Program Criteria:

The architect must be selected by the School Board and chosen from a list of at least six first-rank American architects prepared and submitted by a disinterested panel of two of the country's most distinguished architects.

Competition among architects is encouraged by using a variety of firms. A new or revised list will be submitted for each new building, and the architect selected must be one not previously chosen.

Additions to existing buildings must be designed by the architect of the original structure.

Each architect is required to work within the total budget agreed upon by the School Board.

The architect selected must have the responsibility for planning and designing the total building. This includes recommending landscaping and designing outside areas beyond the entire school area under the park-school plan. In addition, he is responsible for locating the building on site, selecting all colors and recommending all furnishings to be used.

Each architect must be given at least twelve months to plan, design and propose working drawings.

The School Board and the architect chosen execute a standard American Institute of Architects contract form.

The maximum base architectural fee paid by the Foundation shall be determined by a sliding scale established by the AIA based on construction costs. In addition, the Foundation will also contribute 1½% of construction costs for the architect's reimbursable expenses if the firm is east of Denver and 2% if the firm is west of Denver.

The list of buildings whose architecture fees were paid by the Cummins Engine Foundation are:

1957	Lillian C. Schmitt Elementary School
1960	Mabel McDowell Elementary School
1961	Northside Junior High School
1962	Parkside Elementary School
1963	Bartholomew Consolidated School Corporation, Administration Building
1966	W. D. Richards Elementary School
1966	Lincoln Elementary School
1967	Four Seasons Retirement Center
1967	Fire Station No. 4
1969	Southside Junior High School
1969	L. Frances Smith Elementary School
1970	Columbus Post Office
1972	Quinco Consulting Center
1972	Columbus East Senior High School
1972	Mt. Healthy Elementary School
1972	Par 3 Clubhouse
1973	Fodrea Community School

In process:
   City Hall
   Clifty-Petersville Elementary School

This offer was later expanded to include all public buildings on request.

Dedication of
Otter Creek
Club House and
Golf Course, 1964

J. Irwin Miller, Chairman of the Executive and Finance Committee, Cummins Engine Company, Inc.

"Why should an industrial company, organized for profit, think it a good and right thing to take a million dollars, and more, of that profit, and give it to this community in the form of this golf course and club house? Why, instead, isn't Cummins, the largest taxpayer in the county, spending the same energy to try to get its taxes reduced, the cost of education cut, the cost of city government cut, less money spent on streets and utilities and schools?

"This answer is that we would like to see the community come to be not the cheapest community in America, but the very best community of its size in the country. We would like to see it become the city in which the smartest, the ablest, the best young families anywhere would like to live . . . a community that is open in every single respect to persons of every race, color and opinion; that makes them feel welcome and at home here . . . a community which will offer their children the best education available anywhere . . . a community of strong, outspoken churches, of genuine cultural interests, exciting opportunities for recreation . . . a community whose citizens are themselves well paid and who will not tolerate poverty for others, or slums in their midst.

"No such community can be built without citizens determined to make their community best; without city government which works boldly—ahead of its problems, and not always struggling to catch up; and without money sufficient to get the job done.

"So Cummins is not for cheap education, or inadequate, poorly-paid government, or second-rate facilities or low taxes just for the sake of low taxes. Our concern is to help get the most for our dollar, to help build this community into the best in the nation. And we are happy to pay our share, whether in work, or in taxes, or in gifts like this one."

Bruce Adams, New Haven, Connecticut

Major designs:
Fleetguard Office and Manufacturing Building,
    Cookeville, Tennessee

Columbus designs:
Par 3 Golf Course Clubhouse
Cummins Engine Company, Inc., General Office
    Building, Columbus, Indiana
St. Bartholomew Roman Catholic Church
    (Renovation)
Visitors Center (Renovation)

The Architects Collaborative, Inc.
Norman Fletcher, Principal Architect
Cambridge, Massachusetts

Major designs:
American Institute of Architects,
    National Headquarters Building
    Washington, D.C.
Dormitory Quadrangle, Clark University,
    Worcester, Massachusetts
Crown Center Apartments and Condominiums
    Kansas City, Missouri
Brighton Branch Library
    Brighton, Massachusetts

Columbus designs:
Parkside Elementary School
Bartholomew Consolidated School Corporation
    Administration Building
Four Seasons Retirement Center

Edward Larrabee Barnes, New York, New York

Major designs:
Walker Art Center, Minneapolis, Minnesota
Haystack School of Arts and Crafts,
    Deer Isle, Maine
IBM World Trade Headquarters,
    Mount Pleasant, New York
IBM Headquarters at 590 Madison Avenue,
    New York, New York
Christian Theological Seminary
    Indianapolis, Indiana

Columbus design:
W. D. Richards Elementary School

Gunnar Birkerts, Birmingham, Michigan

Major designs:
Federal Reserve Bank of Minneapolis
    Minneapolis, Minnesota
IBM Corporate Computer Center
    Sterling Forest, New York
IBM Office Building
    Southfield, Michigan
Dance Instructional Facility
    Purchase, New York
Tougaloo College Library
    Tougaloo, Mississippi
Corning Museum of Glass
    Corning, New York

Columbus design:
Lincoln Elementary School

Caudill Rowlett Scott
Paul Kennon, Design Partner
Houston, Texas

Major designs:
Solar Energy Research Institute
    Golden, Colorado
IBM Regional Office, Houston, Texas
University of Santa Clara — Student Activity
    Center, Santa Clara, California
Desert Samaritan Hospital, Phoenix, Arizona
Herman Miller, Inc., Chair Manufacturing Plant,
    Holland, Michigan

Columbus designs:
Fodrea Community School, Truitt Garrison,
    Associate Architect
Indiana Bell Telephone Switching Center,
    Jay Bauer, Associate Architect
Irwin Union Bank and Trust Company,
    State and Mapleton Streets,
    Jay Bauer, Associate Architect

Fisher and Spillman Architects, Inc.
Dallas, Texas

Major designs:
College of Fine Arts and Performing Arts Center
    The University of Texas at Austin,
    Austin, Texas
Texas Swimming Center, The University of
    Texas at Austin, Austin, Texas
Tyler Public Library, Tyler, Texas
Dallas Public Library/Central Research Library,
    Dallas, Texas
Texas College of Osteopathic Medicine
    Medical Education Building #1,
    Fort Worth, Texas

Columbus designs:
Irwin Union Bank & Trust Company,
    Taylorsville, Indiana
Foundation For Youth

Gruen Associates, Inc.
Cesar Pelli, Principal Architect
New Haven, Connecticut

Major designs:
Rainbow Center Mall and Winter Garden,
    Niagara Falls, New York
United States Embassy, Tokyo, Japan
Pacific Design Center, Los Angeles, California
Comsat Laboratories, Clarksburg, Maryland

Columbus design:
Commons-Courthouse Center

Hardy Holzman Pfeiffer Associates
New York, New York

Major designs:
Orchestra Hall, Minneapolis, Minnesota
Firemen's Training Center, New York, New York
Brooklyn Children's Museum,
    Brooklyn, New York
Boettcher Concert Hall, Denver, Colorado
Cooper-Hewitt Museum, New York, New York
St. Louis Art Museum, St. Louis, Missouri
Cloisters Condominium, Cincinnati, Ohio
Best Products Corporate Headquarters,
    Richmond, Virginia
Madison Civic Center, Madison, Wisconsin
Dance Studio and Music Performance Hall
    Experimental Theater, St. Paul's School
    Concord, New Hampshire

Columbus designs:
Mt. Healthy Elementary School
Columbus Occupational Health Association

Isaac Hodgson, Indianapolis, Indiana

Major designs:
Courthouse, Marion, Indiana
Polytechnic Institute, Terre Haute, Indiana
Alvord Block, Indianapolis, Indiana
Rose Orphan Asylum, Terre Haute, Indiana
Indiana Female Reformatory, Indianapolis, India
Marion County Courthouse, Indianapolis, Indian

Columbus design:
Bartholomew County Courthouse

John M. Johansen, New York, New York

Major designs:
United States Embassy, Dublin, Ireland
Clowes Memorial Hall & Opera House
    Indianapolis, Indiana
Morris Mechanic Theater, Charles Center
    Baltimore, Maryland
Robert Hutchings Goddard Library,
    Clark University, Worcester, Massachusetts
Oklahoma Theater Center
    Oklahoma City, Oklahoma

Columbus design:
L. Frances Smith Elementary School

Robert Trent Jones, Montclair, New Jersey

Major designs:
Firestone-South Course, Akron, Ohio
Tanglewood Golf Course,
    Winston-Salem, North Carolina
Spyglass Hill, Monterey, California
Hazeltine Course, Minneapolis, Minnesota
Bellerive Course, St. Louis, Missouri

Columbus design:
Otter Creek Golf Course

Dan Kiley, Charlotte, Vermont (Landscaping)

Columbus designs:
Irwin Miller Residence
Clarence Hamilton Residence
Irwin Union Bank & Trust Company
Route #46 Bicentennial Project
Hawcreek Boulevard

Cummins Engine Company, Inc.,
    Technical Center
Cosco, Inc.
North Christian Church
Otter Creek Clubhouse and Golf Course

Richard Meier and Associates
New York, New York

Major designs:
The Atheneum, New Harmony, Indiana
Bronx Development Center,
    New York, New York

Columbus design:
Clifty-Petersville Elementary School

Mitchell-Giurgola Associates
Philadelphia, Pennsylvania

Major designs:
Penn Mutual Tower, Philadelphia, Pennsylvania
Two INA Plaza, Philadelphia, Pennsylvania
University Museum Academic Wing,
    Philadelphia, Pennsylvania
Adult Learning Research Laboratory,
    Bryn Mawr, Pennsylvania

Columbus design:
Columbus East Senior High School

Henry Moore, Much Hadham
Hertfordshire, England (Sculptor)

Major sculptures:
Nuclear Energy, University of Chicago
Reclining Figure, Lincoln Center for the
    Performing Arts, New York

Columbus sculpture:
Large Arch

Eliot Noyes, New Canaan, Connecticut

Major designs:
Mobil Oil Corporation Research and
    Development Center, Princeton, New Jersey
IBM Education Center, Poughkeepsie, New York
IBM Branch Office Buildings, Garden City,
    New York; Hamden, Connecticut and
    Arlington, Virginia

Columbus design:
Southside Junior High School

I. M. Pei and Partners, New York, New York

Major designs:
John Fitzgerald Kennedy Library,
    Boston, Massachusetts
East Building/National Gallery of Art
    Washington, D.C.
John Hancock Tower, Boston, Massachusetts
Spelman Halls, Princeton University,
    Princeton, New Jersey
The Luce Chapel, Taichung, Taiwan

Columbus design:
Cleo Rogers Memorial Library

James Stewart Polshek, New York, New York

Major designs:
New York State Bar Center, Albany, New York
Rosemary Hall/Choate School,
    Wallingford, Connecticut
Kingsborough Community College,
    Brooklyn, New York
Trancas Associates Medical Center (a joint
    venture with Peter L. Gluck, Architect)
    Napa, California
Materials Research Center, Allied Chemical
    Corporation, Morristown, New Jersey

Columbus design:
Quinco Consulting Center

Kevin Roche John Dinkeloo and Associates
Hamden, Connecticut

Major designs:
Oakland Museum, Oakland, California
Ford Foundation Headquarters,
    New York, New York
United Nations Plaza Hotel and Office Building,
    New York, New York
University of Massachusetts Fine Arts Center,
    Amherst, Massachusetts
Deere and Company West Office Building,
    Moline, Illinois

Columbus designs:
Columbus Post Office
Cummins Engine Company, Inc.,
    Components Plant
Irwin Union Bank & Trust Company/Addition

Eero Saarinen, Bloomfield Hills, Michigan

Major designs:
TWA Terminal, Kennedy Airport
John Foster Dulles Airport, Washington, D.C.
Memorial Arch, St. Louis, Missouri
American Embassy, London

Columbus designs:
Irwin Union Bank and Trust Company
North Christian Church

Eliel Saarinen, Bloomfield Hills, Michigan

Major designs:
Art School Buildings, Cranbrook, Michigan
Finnish Pavilion, Paris World Fair
National Museum, Helsinki, Finland

Columbus design:
First Christian Church

Skidmore, Owings & Merrill
Myron Goldsmith, Principal Architect
Chicago, Illinois

Major designs:
60″ Solar Telescope, Kitt Peak, Arizona
St. Joseph Valley Bank Headquarters,
    Elkhart, Indiana
Ruck-A-Chucky Bridge (with T. Y. Lin
    International), Auburn, California
Oakland-Alameda County Coliseum
    Oakland, California

Columbus designs:
The Republic
Central Business District Plan

Charles F. Sparrell, Columbus, Indiana

Columbus designs:
City Hall
First United Methodist Church, 8th and Lafayette
Maple Grove School, 12th and Cottage Avenue
    (Now known as Garfield School)
North Side School, 17th and Home Avenue
    (Now known as McKinley School)

Venturi & Rauch, Philadelphia, Pennsylvania

Major designs:
Franklin Court, Philadelphia, Pennsylvania
Allen Memorial Art Museum Addition,
    Oberlin College, Oberlin, Ohio
Humanities and Social Science Buildings,
    State University of New York,
    Purchase, New York
Institute for Scientific Information,
    Philadelphia, Pennsylvania
Peter Brant House, Greenwich, Connecticut

Columbus design:
Fire Station No. 4

John Carl Warnecke, San Francisco, California

Major designs:
The John F. Kennedy Grave, Arlington National
    Cemetery, Arlington, Virginia
The Hawaii State Capitol, Honolulu, Hawaii
Lafayette Square, Washington, D.C.
Hennepin County Courts, Minneapolis, Minnesota

Columbus design:
Mabel McDowell Elementary School

Harry Weese, Chicago, Illinois

Major designs:
U.S. Embassy, Ghana
IBM Office, Milwaukee, Wisconsin
Northern Baptist Theological Seminary,
    Chicago, Illinois

Columbus designs:
Irwin Union Bank & Trust Company, Hope
    Branch, State Street Office Building,
    Eastbrook Plaza Branch
Lillian C. Schmitt Elementary School
Lincoln Center Ice Skating Rink and Clubhouse
Bartholomew County Home for the Aged
Northside Junior High School
Cosco, Inc., Industrial Plant Offices
Otter Creek Clubhouse and Golf Course
First Baptist Church
Cummins Technical Center
Portions of Cummins Engine Company, Inc., plant
Columbus Village Apartments

Other architects whose works are represented
in this book:

Frank Adams
W. F. Cunn and Company
James Associates
Koster and Associates
McGuire and Shook
Dan Olshavsky
James K. Paris
Henry Phillips
Dean Taylor
Donald G. Wood

Columbus East Senior High School

Mitchell-Giurgola Associates.
Gold Medal, Philadelphia Chapter, American
Institute of Architects: Clarity of its spaces
and the way in which they flow together. 1974

Honor Award, American Institute of Architects:
The clarity and continuity is heightened by its
disciplined use of materials. 1975

Columbus Occupational Health Association

Hardy Holzman Pfeiffer Associates
Honor Award, American Institute of Architects:
Exposes routine medical functions to both
patient and technician which relieves the
tedium of clinical work and the anxiety
of patients. 1976

Bartlett Award, President's Committee for
the Handicapped and American Institute of
Architects: Access and usability for the
handicapped. 1976

Cummins Engine Company
Walesboro Components Plant

Kevin Roche John Dinkeloo and Associates
Exhibit by the Museum of Modern Art, Work in
Progress: Architecture by Philip Johnson, Kevin
Roche, Paul Rudolph. Recognized as prototype
of future factory buildings. 1970

Fodrea Community School

Caudill Rowlett Scott, Paul Kennon and
Truitt Garrison, principal architects.
Outstanding Design Award, American Association of School Administrators: People-oriented
school, flexibility of space. 1972

Award of Excellence, American Iron and
Steel Institute: Best design, low rise
construction. 1975

Honor Award, Texas Society of Architects:
Outstanding architectural design and
achievement. 1975

Award of Excellence, American Institute of
Steel Construction: Outstanding aesthetic
design in structural steel. 1975

Award of Merit, Southern California Chapter,
American Institute of Architects: Excellence in
design and execution. 1975

Indiana Bell Telephone Company
Switching Center

Caudill Rowlett Scott, Paul Kennon, design
principal and Jay Bauer, designer.
Honor Award, Texas Society of Architects:
Lightened a bulky presence in a small residential community. It is an excellent example
of structure as an art form. 1979

Honor Award, American Institute of
Architects. 1980

Landscape Management, Inc.

Columbus, Indiana.
Certificate of Merit, American Association of
Nurserymen for landscaping at Franklin Square
and Irwin Union Bank & Trust Company:
Contributing to the quality of our nation's
environment. 1971

Lincoln Elementary School

Gunnar Birkerts, architect
School of the Month Award, National Council
on Schoolhouse Construction: Freshness,
simplicity and logic of design. 1967

Honor Award, Detroit Chapter, American
Institute of Architects: Coherence of site and
building; thoughtful consistency and directness
of construction. 1968

Honor Award, American Institute of Architects:
Plan section, general development and detailing
. . . very original in quality. 1968

Maschmeyer-Wedco, Inc.

Indiana Award of Merit, Indiana Association
of Nurserymen for landscaping of several
schools in the Bartholomew Consolidated
School Corporation. 1967

Certificate of Merit, American Association of
Nurserymen for landscaping of Irwin Union
Bank and Trust Company. 1971

Mt. Healthy Elementary School

Hardy Holzman Pfeiffer, Hugh Hardy,
principal architect.
Exhibition of School Architecture Commemorative
Plaque, American Association of School Administration and American Institute of Architects:
Commended for its special appeal to young
people. A fun school that surely must be a
great place for learning. 1973

Exhibit at the National Institute of Arts and
Letters. 1974

The Republic

Skidmore, Owings & Merrill, Myron Goldsmith,
principal architect.
First Place Award, Plant Planning Competition
of the American Press Magazine. 1971

Design in Steel Award of the American Iron
and Steel Institute: Excellence in design of
low-rise construction. 1973

Honor Award, American Institute of Architects:
Elegantly proportioned . . . illustrates the vitality
and unlimited variation in the use of structural
expressions as a basis for architectural
forms. 1975

Sandy Hook United Methodist Church

McGuire and Shook Corporation, David
Partenheimer, designer.
Design Award, Indiana Society of Architects:
The way natural light is let into the sanctuary
makes this a grand and moving space, following
the promise of "something special" created
by the spire. 1974

Board of Trustees, Bartholomew Consolidated
School Corporation

Indiana Arts Commission Award: Accepting
the challenge of the community to build
better schools. 1973

City of Columbus
Commemorative plaque by Mrs. Lyndon B.
Johnson during her Crossroads USA Tour
Visit to Columbus in 1967: Recognition of the
community's architectural progress. 1967

Total Design Award, National Society of Interior
Design: Exemplifying environmental rebirth. 1970

Cummins Engine Foundation
Citation of an Organization, American Institute
of Architects: The foundation's efforts have
made Columbus an architectural showcase and
perhaps the best possible example of how
architecture can improve the physical environment and the quality of life. 1975

Mr. and Mrs. J. Irwin Miller
Recognition by the Indiana Association of
Nurserymen: Leadership and foresight in improv-
ing the environment through landscaping. 1972

Thomas Jefferson Award, American Society
of Interior Design: Outstanding dedication
toward preserving America's natural, intellectual
and cultural heritage. 1979

Mr. J. Irwin Miller
Humanitarian Award, National Recreation and
Park Association: Leadership in encouraging
civic improvements in Columbus, including
recreation and educational facilities that few
towns its size can match. 1970

Honorary Member, American Institute of
Architects. 1970

Tiffany Award, Tiffany: Outstanding leadership
of Cummins Engine Company in the field of
industrial design. 1971

Buildings Listed
In National
Register of
Historic Places:

Bartholomew County Historical Museum
1860

Bartholomew County Courthouse
1874

Columbus City Hall
1895

Typography and Design: Paul Rand

Photography: Balthazar Korab

Contributing Orlando Cabanban
Photographers: Jon Carlson
Francis O. Galbraith
Hedrick-Blessing
Norman McGrath
David Neuman
Virgil Parker

Printer: The Avery Press, Inc.